NOAH'S 20th CENTURY ARK

— Susan Miller

UNDERSTANDING & CREATING EDITORIAL CARTOONS

A RESOURCE BOOK

Knowledge Unlimited PO Box 52 Madison, WI 53701
Copyright © 1998

INTRODUCTION

The Editorial Cartoon as a Teaching Tool

This resource book contains 54 individual student activity sheets and a great many other suggestions for using editorial cartoons in the classroom.

This book will help your students learn to draw their own editorial cartoons, but that isn't its main objective. If it were, we would have included more material on artistic technique. Instead, the book is primarily designed to help you use editorial cartoons as a teaching tool.

Editorial cartoons are a unique way to present ideas. Obviously, they are expressions of opinion. But a political slogan on a sign or a poster is also an expression of opinion. Editorial cartoons, at their best, are much more: They are arguments about important issues in the news. And they are meant to provoke thought, not merely assert a position. As such, they engage the reader actively in a debate. Editorial cartoons make use of many of the ideas and concepts of the social studies and language arts curricula. And they assume in the reader an understanding of and ability to apply these ideas and concepts.

For example, many editorial cartoons include historical figures, important historical events, or famous sayings that relate the past to the present in complex and subtle ways. Others assume knowledge of geography, economics, international relations, government and more. Most editorial cartoons implicitly theorize about cause-and-effect relationships among events and trends. They certainly force the reader to sharpen skills at spotting bias. And they call on those readers to use their knowledge of society to form their own opinions, make judgments, and take action as citizens.

Editorial cartoons also make dramatic use of many important literary devices, such as symbols, exaggeration, and irony. And understanding how editorial cartoons work requires students to understand the visual narrative form. In other words, in a unique, pleasing, and visual way, editorial cartoons can foster many of the important intellectual skills teachers want to develop in their students.

Some of the most cleverly executed editorial cartoons appear to be very simple. But learning to understand and create these cartoons is no easy task. Any good editorial cartoon — even a very simple one — is made up of several elements. To fully understand such cartoons requires skill at deciphering a complex code of symbols, shadings, caricature, line, and much more. Words play a part, but only in relation to the visual elements. With the help of the materials in this book, your students will learn to "read" the language of editorial cartoons. And through the activities in each section, they can learn to use this language to express their own insights about the important issues affecting all of us as citizens of the nation and the world.

PUBLISHED BY KNOWLEDGE UNLIMITED® INC. PO BOX 52 MADISON, WI 53701
(608) 836-6660 ■ (800) 356-2303
www.knowledgeunlimited.com

UNDERSTANDING & CREATING EDITORIAL CARTOONS © 1998 by Knowledge Unlimited® Inc. All Rights Reserved.
ISBN 1-55933-015-5
Student activity sheets may be duplicated for classroom use.

Contents

Section 1
Understanding the Cartoon's Main Idea 1

Section 2
Analogy & Symbol 10

Section 3
Humor & Irony 20

Section 4
Exaggeration & Understatement 32

Section 5
Caricature & Stereotype 43

Section 6
Captions & Other Words 53

Section 7
Drawing & Design 65

Section 8
Literary & Historical References 76

Section 9
Cartoons & History 87

Bibliography..................96

Suggestions for Using This Resource Book

This resource book is divided into nine sections, each of which deals with one aspect of editorial cartooning.

EACH SECTION CONTAINS THE FOLLOWING:

- A definition of an instructional objective.

- Comments on the nature and importance of a single aspect of editorial cartooning. You may use the comments in this essay as a guide for a teacher-directed discussion. Student and professionally drawn editorial cartoons illustrating the points in the essay are included in an easy-to-reproduce form.

- Six individual student activity sheets, also in an easy-to-reproduce form. The activities in each section appear in approximate order of increasing difficulty. We encourage you to look at all the activities, however; the simpler ones may be quite appropriate for students who are also able to use the more advanced ones. And, with modifications, the more complex activities may work for less advanced students.

This book is designed for maximum flexibility. If your class works its way through all the sections here, your students will come away with a much better understanding of how editorial cartoons work and how to draw their own. However, the lessons in this book may also be used independently so that you may focus on any of the concepts addressed here.

Once you've completed the lessons in this book, why not see how your students fare as editorial cartoonists? Each year, Knowledge Unlimited sponsors a Student Editorial Cartoon Contest in conjunction with the NewsCurrents current events discussion program. To find out more information about this contest, or about NewsCurrents, call (800) 356-2303, write us at Knowledge Unlimited, PO Box 52, Madison, WI 53701, or look us up on our Web site www.knowledgeunlimited.com.

SECTION 1

UNDERSTANDING THE CARTOON'S MAIN IDEA

OBJECTIVES

The activities in this section are designed to help your students understand the editorial cartoon as a unified, visual expression of a single opinion or idea about a public issue in the news. These activities are also designed to help students improve their ability to identify the main idea in any complicated message.

COMMENTS

An editorial cartoon exists to make a point about some issue in the news. The very first thing students must realize about drawing editorial cartoons is that you need to start with a single, clear idea. You do not have to be a great artist to draw an effective editorial cartoon. But you *do* need to understand the issue you are addressing and you must know precisely what point you wish to make about that issue.

The most common problem with student editorial cartoons is a lack of clarity about what the cartoons are saying. All too often, a necessary element is missing or an unnecessary (and distracting) element is present — not because the student is a poor artist, but because he or she is not clear about what the cartoon's point is. It is important for a student to think through the issue he or she is going to illustrate before drawing anything.

In one sense, it is probably easy to state the main idea of most editorial cartoons. Take a look, for example at the cartoons on the next pages. Cartoon #1 is obviously about the problem of violence in American. It's possible to be even more specific and say it is about how terrified Americans have become about street crime.

But even this more narrowed-down statement isn't what we mean when we talk about the main idea of a cartoon. What we have in mind is a single statement that takes into account all of the cartoon's unique elements, a statement that sums up what that cartoon, as opposed to all others, is saying. After all, the phrase "Americans are frightened about street crime," could apply equally to Cartoon #2.

In order to truly understand editorial cartoons, students need to learn to state a cartoon's main idea or point in a way that accounts for all of that cartoon's elements, and that distinguishes that cartoon from all others. For each cartoon does differ from every other one, however subtly. And it is in those differences that the cartoon's real message is contained.

The best cartoons are not literal. This is a point you will want to stress over and over to your students. If a cartoon were literal (if for example it could be completely summed up in some direct statement such as, "Russia is having a lot of trouble changing from communism to capitalism.") what would be the point of turning that literal statement into a cartoon? It is the visual medium that allows the cartoonist to tease the viewer with an idea and to force the viewer to use his or her imagination.

Ask your students to try to write a one-or-two sentence definition of the point that each of the two cartoons on the following page are making. But be sure the definition they give for one cartoon can't be mistaken as a definition for the other. This exercise should convince them that editorial cartoons are only superficially "simple" art forms. And you'll see the importance of identifying the one central idea at the heart of each cartoon.

Section 1 — Understanding the Cartoon's Main Idea

CARTOON #1

Section 1 — Understanding the Cartoon's Main Idea

CARTOON #2

Understanding the Cartoon's Main Idea 3

Section 1 — Understanding the Cartoon's Main Idea — Activity #1

Find an editorial cartoon in your newspaper. Attach it here. Then answer the questions below.

Name of the cartoonist _____

Name of the newspaper. _____

In one sentence, explain the main point of this cartoon. _____
_____
_____
_____

Section 1 — Understanding the Cartoon's Main Idea — Activity #2

A newspaper headline is meant to tell the main idea of the story. Clip a news story that interests you and attach it to this sheet. Now use the story's headline as a caption for a cartoon. Draw a cartoon here to fit with that headline-caption.

Understanding the Cartoon's Main Idea

Section 1 — Understanding the Cartoon's Main Idea — Activity #3

Look through the newspaper for news stories about important events in the nation or the world. Pick five of these stories. Circle what seems to be the single most important sentence in each story. Now choose one of those stories. Attach it here. In the space provided, use the single sentence from the article you chose as a cartoon caption and draw a cartoon illustrating the main idea of the news story.

_____

_____

_____

_____

Section 1 — Understanding the Cartoon's Main Idea — Activity #4

Find an editorial cartoon in your daily newspaper. Attach the cartoon here and answer the questions below.

Name the artist who drew the cartoon, the newspaper in which it appeared, and the date on which it appeared.
_____
_____

What is the cartoon's subject? That is, what issue, news story, or problem is the cartoon about?
_____
_____

In a brief paragraph on a separate sheet of paper, explain the main point the cartoon is making about its subject.
_____
_____
_____
_____
_____
_____
_____

Section 1 — Understanding the Cartoon's Main Idea — Activity #5

With the best cartoons, the main idea is rarely stated directly and obviously in words, either as a title or a caption or in any other way. If it were, the viewer wouldn't have to think about the visual elements in the cartoon. By themselves, the words in this cartoon do NOT express the cartoon's main idea. To understand that idea you need to look closely at all the elements in the cartoon. After studying the cartoon, answer the questions about it below.

In a sentence or two, what is the cartoon's main point? _____

How do the piano keys help to make that point in an ironic way? _____

What other features in the cartoon help it make its point? _____

8

Understanding & Creating Editorial Cartoons

Section 1 — Understanding the Cartoon's Main Idea — Activity #6

Some cartoons are simple. Others are quite complicated. But no matter how complex, a cartoon must make one clear statement about something. This student editorial cartoon is visually complicated. But it does have one main point. Study it closely. Then answer the questions below.

What is the cartoon's main point? _____
_____
_____

Why do you think the artist included so many reporters in the interview on the left side of the cartoon? _____
_____
_____

Why is it unlikely that, in real life, the figures labeled "Sharpton" and "Farrakhan" would be with the others on the right? _____
_____
_____

Without the "Sharpton" and "Farrakhan" figures in that group, the cartoon's point would change. How? _____
_____
_____
_____

Understanding the Cartoon's Main Idea

Section 2

Analogy & Symbol

OBJECTIVES

The activities in this section are designed to help your students understand what analogies and symbols in cartoons are, and — more importantly — why they are the essential ingredients that make cartoons thought-provoking forms of expression.

COMMENTS

What makes an editorial cartoon more than a simple literal statement of an opinion or idea is its use of analogy, symbol, or metaphor. The strength of an editorial cartoon lies in analogy. The best editorial cartoonists do not depict a problem in literal terms. They liken it to something else and invite the reader to stretch his or her imagination.

In this section, it is important to teach students exactly what an analogy is, and why it has the power to stretch the imagination and make us think. In its simplest terms, an analogy says, "this thing is like that other thing, at least in one respect."

Look at the cartoons on the next few pages. In Cartoon #1, the idea of disease is shown as a monster that is swallowing up a demonstrator opposed to the use of animals in medical lab experiments. In Cartoon #2, the nation's health care system is shown as a sick patient. A program to reform health care is shown as some medicine being fed into the patient's arm. But the high cost of the program is symbolized by the blood dripping from the patient's other arm. Obviously, no analogy is perfect. Money is not blood. But the two may be alike in some ways. In what ways? That's for you, as the reader of the cartoon, to figure out.

Symbols are the elements that make up most analogies. They may be unique. Or they may be widely shared and recognized — Uncle Sam, the Republican elephant, etc. Analogies and symbols in cartoons present abstract ideas or problems in a visual form. In doing this, they give the mind a handle, a way into a subject. They enable us to grasp what we can't see. They extend thought. In a way, all human language and thought has evolved through just such imaginative extensions of one idea to another.

To get a bit more down to earth, take a look at Cartoon #3, a student-drawn cartoon. The analogies in this cartoon are fairly simple. Crime is a powerful bulldog, the rest of society is a helpless cat, and a weak system of justice is a broken chain. Yet, think of how much more this cartoon conveys than a statement such as, "Crime is destroying our society." The bulldog evokes a range of meanings and strong feelings of something dangerous, something with a life of its own, something massive and unpredictable, etc.

Obviously, crime isn't exactly like this bulldog. In fact, it could be maintained that this symbol exaggerates the problem and makes us think about it in distorted ways. But even if that's so, isn't it a valuable exercise to have to think through the point of similarity and difference between this analogy and the thing it stands for?

Your students can begin to learn to do just that by trying some of the exercises in this section.

Section 2 — Analogy & Symbol

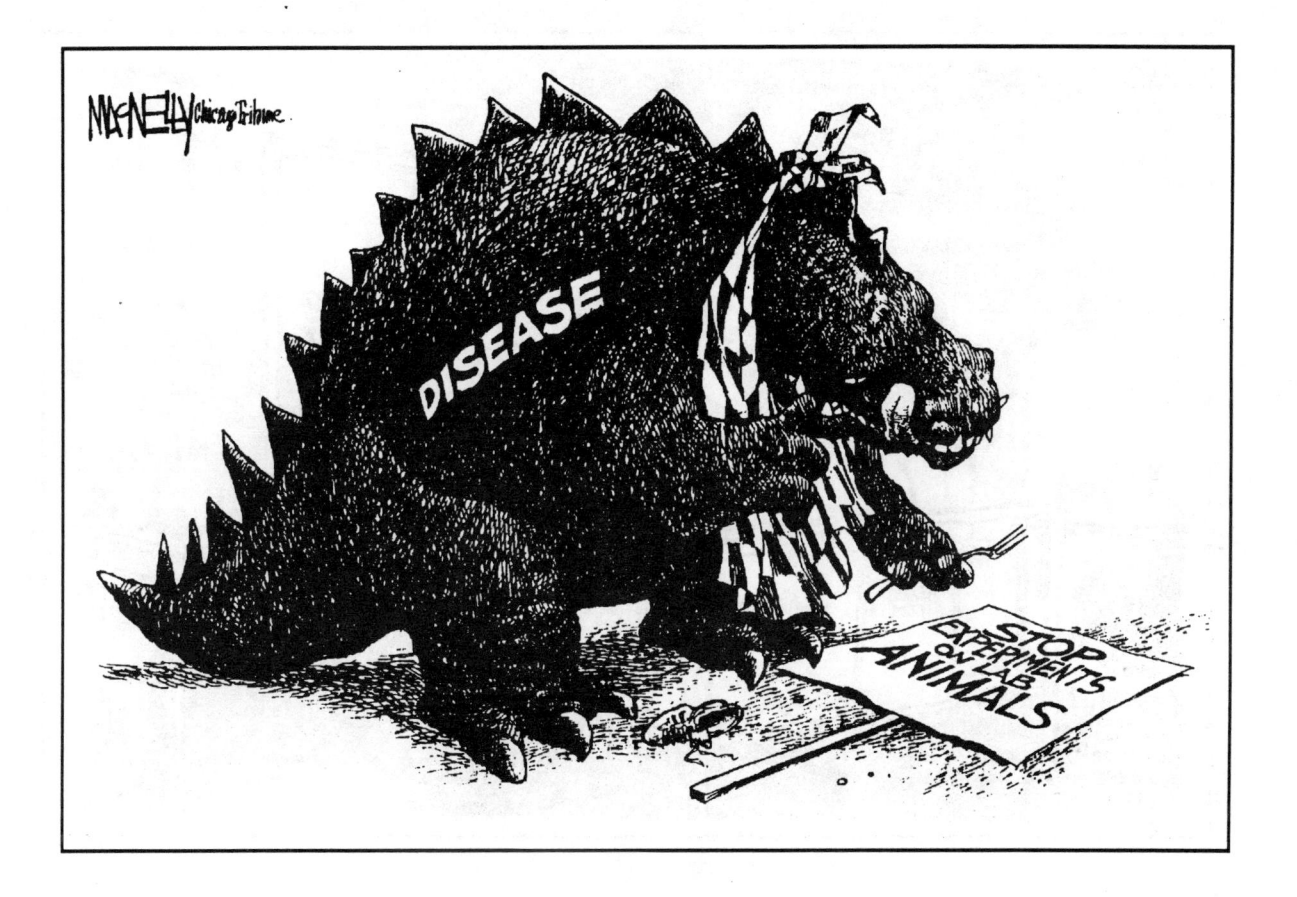

CARTOON #1

Section 2 — Analogy & Symbol

CARTOON #2

Understanding & Creating Editorial Cartoons

Section 2 — Analogy & Symbol

CARTOON #3

Section 2 — Analogy & Symbol — Activity #1

Most cartoons use symbols — that is, objects or designs that stand for some other thing or idea. This cartoon uses symbols to make its point. Study the cartoon. Then answer the questions below.

How many symbols can you find in this cartoon? _____
_____
_____

What do the markings on the inside of the tire and on the air pump mean? _____
_____
_____

What is the cartoon's main point?_____
_____
_____

14   Understanding & Creating Editorial Cartoons

Section 2 — Analogy & Symbol — Activity #2

Many cartoons use an elephant for the Republican Party and a donkey for the Democratic Party. Below is a list of animals and a list of people or problems in the news. Draw a line connecting each item on the right to the animal you think would be the best symbol for it.

tiger	the president
dog	harmful drugs
monkey	war
dinosaur	Congress
turtle	the deficit
peacock	students

Now use some of these symbols in a cartoon about some problem in the news. Draw your cartoon in the space below.

Analogy & Symbol

Section 2 — Analogy & Symbol — Activity #3

Editorial cartoonists often use figures from fables or children's stories in their cartoons. For example, many cartoons use the figures of the wolf and Little Red Riding Hood. In these cartoons, the wolf stands for some problem or someone who is bad. Little Red Riding Hood stands for someone who is being fooled or tricked.

Below are five suggested names for the wolf and five for Little Red Riding Hood. Choose one name for each figure and draw your own cartoon about an issue or problem that involves these two people or groups. Show one of these people or groups as the wolf and the other as Little Red Riding Hood. Add words to show what the figures are saying. The point of your cartoon will depend on how you label each of the two figures and what you have each of them say. As a group, share and discuss your cartoons.

WOLF	LITTLE RED RIDING HOOD
Congress	the public
terrorists	airplane passengers
news reporters	the president
corporations	news reporters
the president	taxpayers

Section 2 — Analogy & Symbol — Activity #4

Many cartoons use famous symbols simply as a way to identify parts of the cartoon — for example, Uncle Sam to stand for the United States. Each of these two cartoons uses a well-known symbol in a more complicated way. Study these cartoons closely. Then answer the questions below.

What symbol does each cartoon use, and what does that symbol usually stand for? _____
_____
_____

How does the artist use the symbol not only to stand for something, but to help the cartoon make its main point? _____
_____
_____

Analogy & Symbol

Section 2 — Analogy & Symbol — Activity #5

This cartoon uses the relationship between a rickety old airplane and a dotted line showing the plane's path of flight to make a point about U.S. schools and the academic performance of their students. In other words, the plane and the dotted line are used as an analogy for the school system and student achievement. Below are a number of other relationships that might have been used as analogies in a cartoon about the same topic. Choose one of these pairs and use it to draw your own cartoon about this topic.

> fire truck and fire
> sinking ship and life boats
> hospital and patient
> pool table and billiard balls
> airplane and parachutes
> hunter and ducks

Understanding & Creating Editorial Cartoons

Section 2 — Analogy & Symbol — Activity #6

Newspaper editorials often use analogies and metaphors to express abstract ideas about news events, issues, and personalities. Here are a few examples: "This greatest of American leadership has been replaced by a wrecking crew." "But neither Congress nor the Administration wants real cuts; they want monkey business." "Every time the Judicial Commission pops its head out of its foxhole, people start taking shots at it."

During the next week, read all the editorials and columns on your newspaper's editorial page. In the space below, record all the statements you find that use symbols, analogies, or metaphors. Create an editorial cartoon that uses some of these images to make the same point as one of the editorials you have read.

SECTION 3

HUMOR & IRONY

OBJECTIVES

Satire and irony are the main forms of humor in most editorial cartoons. The activities in this section should help students get some idea of what these kinds of humor are and how they can help a cartoon make its point more effectively.

COMMENTS

Examine the cartoons on the pages that follow. Cartoon #1, drawn by a high school student, makes it clear that an editorial cartoon need not be humorous to make a powerful statement in an effective way.

But it isn't easy to make a completely humorless cartoon work. In the world of ideas, the editorial cartoon is already a kind of blunt instrument. A grimly serious cartoon always is in danger of being heavy-handed. To be effective, it needs to give the reader an honorable way out. An editorial cartoon must respect its dissenters enough to avoid implying that they are either fools or knaves simply for disagreeing.

Serious as it is, Cartoon #1 is quite effective. It wouldn't have worked well had the words in it read, "The death penalty violates one of the Ten Commandments." Instead, the cartoon simply lets the Commandment speak for itself. That way, each reader is allowed to decide what the cartoon's implications are.

In a great many cases, humor is the primary means by which a cartoon gives the reader that kind of space. The humor may be subtle, as in Cartoon #2.

It may be satirical, poking fun at lawmakers or other easily recognizable public targets, as in Cartoon #3.

Or it may be biting and ironic, as in Cartoon #4, about oil spills.

Irony is an especially effective form of humor for editorial cartoons. Its essence is to use words (or some other feature in the cartoon) to express a meaning contrary to the overall point the cartoon is actually trying to make. This disharmony adds to the task of interpreting the cartoon, and this forces the reader to become even more of an active participant in the "dialogue" the cartoon initiates.

In a great many cartoons, humor is produced by taking a line of thought, or a trend in society, to its logical, but absurd, conclusion. In other cartoons, the humor is of the "laughing to keep from crying" variety as with Cartoon #5. This cartoon also proves that even a dismal subject can inspire a humorous and thought-provoking cartoon.

Section 3 — Humor & Irony

CARTOON #1

Section 3 — Humor & Irony

CARTOON #2

Section 3 — Humor & Irony

CARTOON #3

Section 3 — Humor & Irony

CARTOON #4

24   Understanding & Creating Editorial Cartoons

Section 3 —Humor & Irony

CARTOON #5

Section 3 — Humor & Irony — Activity #1

Editorial cartoons often try to make us laugh about very serious problems or dangers in our world. Look through recent newspapers for examples of editorial cartoons you think are funny. Attach two of them in the space provided here. Then answer the questions below.

Which cartoon is funniest? _____
_____
_____

Which cartoon makes its point best? _____
_____
_____

Which cartoon do you like best? Why? _____
_____
_____

Section 3 — Humor & Irony — Activity #2

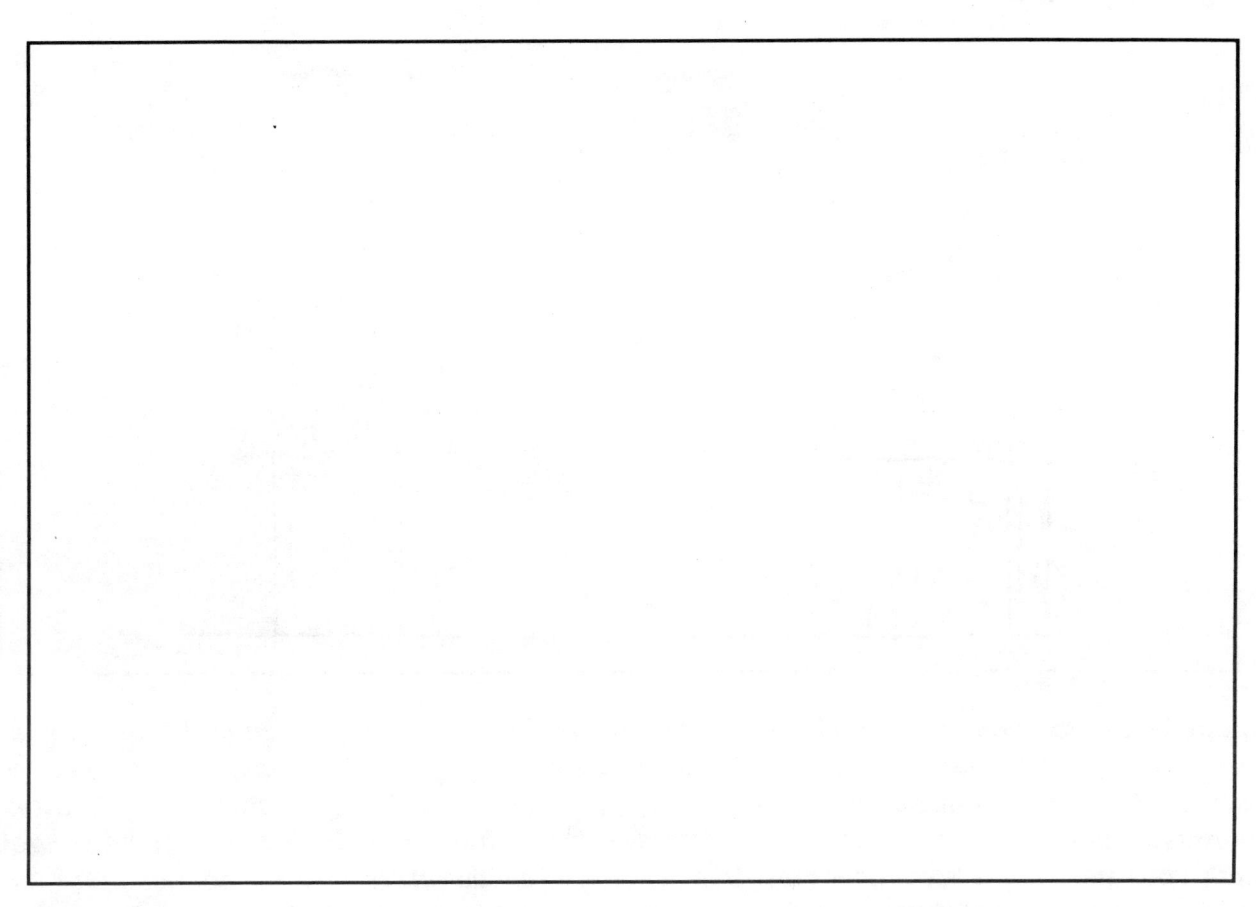

One way to make a funny cartoon is to make a serious photograph into a cartoon by using word or thought balloons the way comic strips do. Find a photo in your newspaper that shows two or more people. Attach the word and thought balloons to it. Make a funny cartoon by adding words to the balloons. Attach your photo-cartoon in the space above.

Humor & Irony

27

Section 3 — Humor & Irony — Activity #3

Speech bubble: "I knew Garfield, and you're not Garfield"

Desks labeled: Snoopy | Heathcliff

During a debate in 1988 between vice presidential candidates Lloyd Bentsen and Dan Quayle, Mr. Bentsen made fun of some remarks Mr. Quayle made about former President John Kennedy. Mr. Bentsen said, "I knew John Kennedy, and you are no John Kennedy." The above student editorial cartoon uses two famous comic strip characters to take a humorous look at that debate. Look through your newspaper's comic strips. Use some of the characters in these comics in a humorous cartoon of your own about a recent news story. Draw your cartoon in the space below.

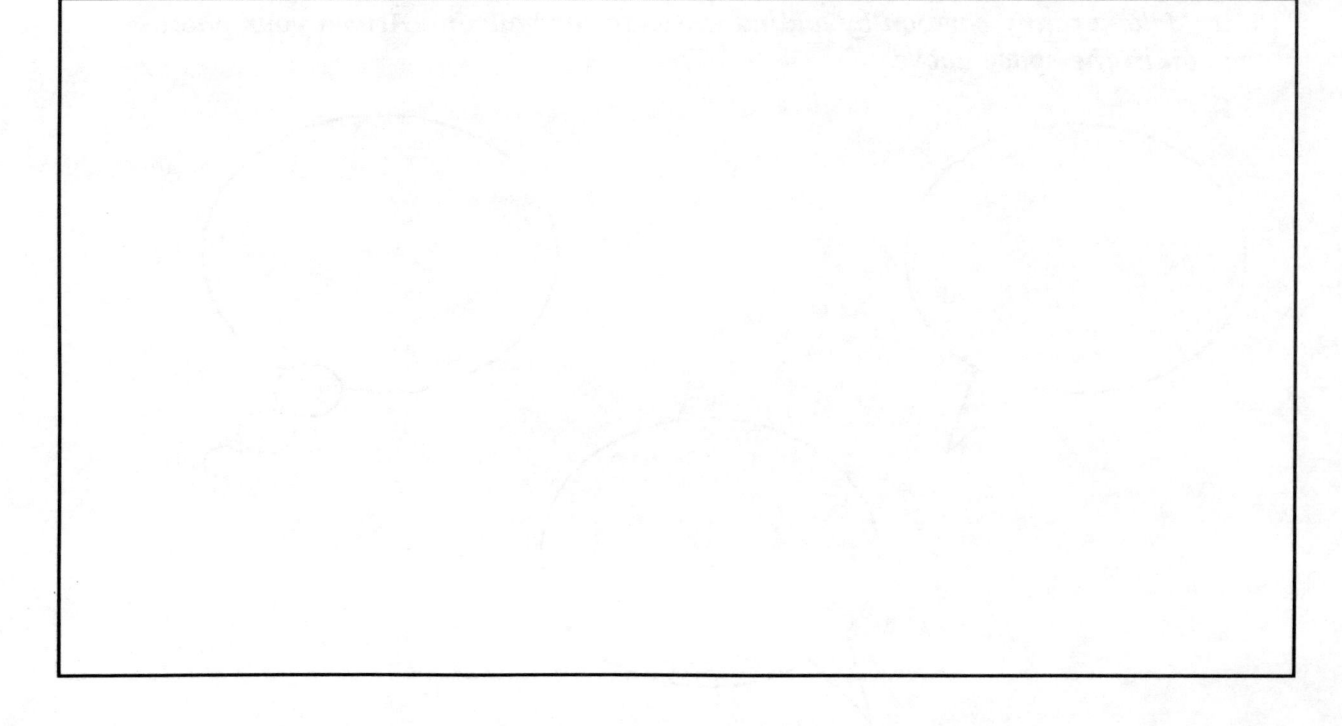

Section 3 — Humor & Irony — Activity #4

Advertisements can give you ideas for funny cartoons. Find an ad in a newspaper or magazine. Attach the ad here. In the space below, use the picture in the ad to draw a funny cartoon about some local, national, or world news event.

ADVERTISEMENT

YOUR CARTOON

Humor & Irony

29

Section 3 — Humor & Irony — Activity #5

Both of these editorial cartoons comment on the problems of guns and violence. The cartoon on the left uses humor. The other cartoon is not humorous. Study the two cartoons closely. Then answer the questions below.

Summarize in a sentence or two the different points each cartoon makes about guns. _____
_____
_____
_____

What techniques in the cartoon on the left make it humorous? _____
_____
_____

Which cartoon do you like best? Why? _____
_____
_____

30   Understanding & Creating Editorial Cartoons

Section 3 — Humor & Irony — Activity #6

On your newspaper's editorial page, find an editorial or column on some serious issue in the news today. Underline all the opinion words in the editorial or column. Now circle all the adjectives or descriptive phrases that emphasize the point the writer is making. Based on the opinions expressed in the editorial or column, draw two editorial cartoons in the space provided below. In one cartoon, make the writer's point in a serious, humorless way. In the other, make it in a humorous way. As a group, share the cartoons and decide which ones are most effective.

SERIOUS CARTOON

HUMOROUS CARTOON

Humor & Irony

31

SECTION 4

EXAGGERATION & UNDERSTATEMENT

OBJECTIVES

The activities in this section are designed to help your students understand the role exaggeration, visual hyperbole, and excessive understatement play in helping a cartoon get its point across. In particular, students should come to appreciate the way in which exaggeration and the relative proportions of objects in a cartoon can be used to visually illustrate many kinds of relationships — of strength, speed, size, importance, etc.

COMMENTS

Exaggeration is what gives an editorial cartoon its punch. In the world of journalism, editorial cartoons are sledgehammers. They have to capture a reader's attention and hammer home a point in a matter of seconds. A cartoon may have a complex and subtle message to deliver. But unless it grabs the reader and forces a response, that complexity is going to be wasted

By outrageously exaggerating or understating something, a cartoon does engage in a kind of deliberate artistic distortion of the truth. But if done correctly, that distortion will be for a good cause. It will help provoke debate and force the reader to think in a more concentrated way about an issue.

Two points should be made clear to students. First, there are many ways to use exaggeration or understatement in a cartoon. Secondly, not all forms of exaggeration work.

Take a look at the cartoons on the pages that follow. Most obviously, exaggeration takes the form of changes in the normal proportions between objects, as in Cartoon #1, a student cartoon.

Or a cartoon may exaggerate the seriousness of the problem addressed as in the case in Cartoon #2, which pokes fun at the poor showing of Americans on tests of geography knowledge.

In Cartoon #3, another student-drawn cartoon, the seriousness of a problem's consequences has been exaggerated.

The impact of a cartoon's exaggeration can sometimes be heightened by combining it with the ironic use of understatement. In Cartoon #4, the calm, casual exchange between the teacher and the students adds to the impact of the exaggerated portrayal of the problem of violence in schools.

All the forms of exaggeration in these cartoons work well. But there is a fine line between effective exaggeration and silliness. A cartoon that does nothing more than blow out of proportion the seriousness or danger of some problem may only provoke disbelief. If the cartoon screams out about a problem that is truly dangerous, that's one thing. But in many cases, it's better to add some kind of light touch to a cartoon. In Cartoon #3 (the Greenhouse Effect cartoon), the surfer, the question mark over the polar bear's head, and the understated caption all provide that light touch.

To sum up, your students need to understand that editorial cartoons are indeed sledgehammers — but gentle sledgehammers.

Section 4 — Exaggeration & Understatement

CARTOON #1

Exaggeration & Understatement 33

Section 4 — Exaggeration & Understatement

CARTOON #2

Section 4 — Exaggeration & Understatement

CARTOON #3

Exaggeration & Understatement

Section 4 — Exaggeration & Understatement

CARTOON #4

36 Understanding & Creating Editorial Cartoons

Section 4 — Exaggeration & Understatement — Activity #1

The cartoon below uses exaggeration. Look at it closely. Then answer the questions underneath it.

What object in the cartoon is shown very large? _____
_____
_____
_____

What does this object stand for? _____
_____
_____
_____

What objects are small? _____
_____
_____
_____

What do these objects stand for? _____
_____
_____
_____

What point does the cartoon make? _____
_____
_____
_____

Exaggeration & Understatement

Section 4 — Exaggeration & Understatement — Activity #2

Cartoons don't always exaggerate things by showing them as very large or very small. Sometimes the exaggeration is in how a problem is presented, how much money it will cost to solve it, and so on. The student cartoon below exaggerates something in this way. Study it closely. Then answer the questions below.

"HAVE A GOOD DAY AT SCHOOL JIMMY!"

In a sentence or two, what big problem is this cartoon about? _____
_____
_____
_____
_____
_____
_____

In what way does the cartoon exaggerate the problem? _____
_____
_____
_____
_____
_____
_____
_____

Understanding & Creating Editorial Cartoons

Section 4 — Exaggeration & Understatement — Activity #3

Both of the cartoons below use exaggeration to make points about the same problem. Look at the two cartoons closely. Then answer the following questions.

What in the cartoon on the left is exaggerated? _____
_____
_____
_____
_____

What in the cartoon on the right is exaggerated? _____
_____
_____
_____
_____

Which cartoon do you think makes the best use of exaggeration? Why? _____
_____
_____
_____
_____

Exaggeration & Understatement

Section 4 — Exaggeration & Understatement — Activity #4

Below is a list of problems in the news. What object or group of objects would you use in an editorial cartoon to stand for each problem listed? Next to each problem, write the name of the object or objects you would use.

political scandals _____
_____
_____
_____

terrorism _____
_____
_____
_____

pollution _____
_____
_____
_____

school violence _____
_____
_____
_____

racial prejudice _____
_____
_____
_____

Now read more about one of these problems. On separate sheets of paper, draw two editorial cartoons using the object or objects you have chosen for that problem. In one cartoon exaggerate the way you draw the object or objects in some way. In the other, do not exaggerate them. Which cartoon do you think is better?

Section 4 — Exaggeration & Understatement — Activity #5

This cartoon uses hyperbole, or exaggeration, to make its point. But it also uses a humorous kind of understatement — in the expressions on the faces of the gun store owner and the customer, for example. Study the cartoon closely. Then answer the questions below.

In a sentence or two, what is the cartoon's main point? _____
_____
_____
_____

In what way does the cartoon use exaggeration to make its point? _____
_____
_____
_____

How do the expressions on the faces of the gun store owner and the customer add to the cartoon's overall impact? _____
_____
_____

Do you see any other examples of understatement here? If so, what are they? How do they add to the cartoon's point? _____
_____
_____

Exaggeration & Understatement 41

Section 4 — Exaggeration & Understatement — Activity #6

Cartoons exaggerate certain features — either in terms of their size or in some other way — in order to make a point effectively and dramatically. But exaggeration can also unfairly distort the nature of the problem the cartoon addresses. In this cartoon, a huge crocodile is used to make a strong point about negotiating with terrorists. Study the cartoon. Then write a brief answer to each of the two questions below.

[Cartoon: A person seated in an armchair inside the gaping jaws of an enormous crocodile, saying "WE LOOK FORWARD TO DISCUSSIONS WHICH WE HOPE WILL BE FRANK AND OPEN..." Caption: "NEGOTIATING WITH TERRORISTS."]

A person who agrees with this cartoon's point would say the exaggeration in it is justified because. . . _____

_____
_____
_____
_____
_____

A person who disagrees with the cartoon's point would say the exaggeration in it is distorted because. . . _____

_____
_____
_____
_____
_____

Understanding & Creating Editorial Cartoons

SECTION 5

CARICATURE & STEREOTYPE

OBJECTIVES

The activities in this section are designed to help students better appreciate the role of caricatures and stereotypes in editorial cartooning. The activities will show students that caricature is more than a way to exaggerate and make fun of well-known figures in the news. In conjunction with other cartoon elements, caricature can deepen the impact and reinforce the message of an editorial cartoon. Students should also come to recognize the value of stereotypes in a cartoon, as well as their limitations and their potential to reinforce simple-minded and harmful prejudices.

COMMENTS

The cartoons on the following pages illustrate some of the uses of caricature and stereotype in an editorial cartoon. Caricature is what makes the well-known figures in a cartoon immediately recognizable. That is perhaps caricature's most obvious function in editorial cartooning. Clearly that's the job caricature is doing in Cartoon #1, an editorial cartoon about Cuba's Fidel Castro.

In other words, given that a cartoon is not a photographic medium, caricature helps us identify a news figure quickly. It usually does this by exaggerating or distorting one or more of that person's prominent features.

But caricature is used for more than simple identification purposes. Editorial cartoons generally aim to stir up emotions and provoke debate. To do this, they attack, needle, deflate, and ridicule. On the whole, caricatures are not flattering. And the features cartoonists choose to exaggerate in the caricatures they draw are almost always the least flattering — Richard Nixon's five-o-clock shadow, Bill Clinton's round nose, Lyndon Johnson's big ears and squinty eyes.

At its best, caricatures can reveal inner strengths and weakness of character. This is certainly true of many of the works of caricaturist David Levine, about whom one writer has said, "David has the wit, taste, and genius to sense exactly how far to sink his teeth into the essence of a subject without losing credibility or lapsing into polemical farce. Moreover, his work invariably serves to expand our knowledge of the subject, not simply as to features but to something of the person beneath."

And as Cartoon #2 proves, even fairly simple caricatures can be used to do much more than simply identify or ridicule prominent people. The use of caricature in this cartoon allows it to make a complex and subtle comparison of the presidential styles of Ronald Reagan and Theodore Roosevelt.

In a way, stereotypes are the opposite of caricatures. They obscure or eliminate anything uniquely individual by exaggerating features associated with an entire group. In doing this, they often play on unconscious biases we all share. For the cartoonist, they are a great convenience — the bearded protester, the pipe-smoking professor, the bent and stooped social security recipient. But they can be misleading — and insulting.

Still, it's not always easy to tell whether a given stereotype is simply a quick and easy way to communicate or a demeaning slur on some group. The one in Cartoon #3 could easily be called demeaning. And if you are a member of Congress, you're likely to find the one in Cartoon #4 highly insulting.

As your students learn to be more aware of these cartooning devices, they will be better prepared to make individual judgments about the cartoons they see. In the activities that follow, we'll ask your students to exercise their critical thinking skills as they consider the elements of caricature and stereotype.

Caricature & Stereotype

Section 5 — Caricature & Stereotype

THE OLD GUNFIGHTER

CARTOON #1

44   Understanding & Creating Editorial Cartoons

Section 5 — Caricature & Stereotype

CARTOON #2

Caricature & Stereotype

45

Section 5 — Caricature & Stereotype

CARTOON #3

Section 5 — Caricature & Stereotype

CARTOON #4

Caricature & Stereotype 47

Section 5 — Caricature & Stereotype — Activity #1

A caricature is a drawing of someone that exaggerates certain features of that person. These drawings are caricatures of the famous people listed below.

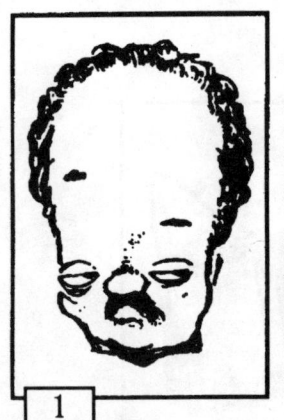

| 1 | 2 | 3 | 4 | 5 |

Match each name with the number next to his caricature. Then in each case, list the feature or features in the caricature that are exaggerated or made to look silly.

	NUMBER	FEATURES EXAGGERATED
Jesse Jackson	_____	_____
Ronald Reagan	_____	_____
Albert Einstein	_____	_____
James Madison	_____	_____
Franklin Roosevelt	_____	_____

Which of these caricatures do you like best? Why? _____
_____
_____
_____
_____
_____
_____

Understanding & Creating Editorial Cartoons

Section 5 — Caricature & Stereotype — Activity #2

Find a photograph of a well-known person in the news. That person could be from your own community or state, from somewhere else in the nation, or from another country. Attach the photo of this person in the space here. Using the photo, draw your own caricature in the other space. Remember to exaggerate a main feature or element in this person's appearance.

PHOTOGRAPH

YOUR CARICATURE

Caricature & Stereotype

Section 5 — Caricature & Stereotype — Activity #3

Caricatures often exaggerate the unusual features of a person's face — for example, Ronald Reagan's wavy hair or Bill Clinton's chin. The photograph on the left is of Supreme Court Justice Antonin Scalia. Using this photo as a guide, draw your own caricature of Mr. Scalia in the space provided on the right.

Read newspaper stories about Justice Scalia and his views on some issue before the Supreme Court. In the space below, use your caricature in a cartoon about one of these issues.

Understanding & Creating Editorial Cartoons

Section 5 — Caricature & Stereotype — Activity #4

Harnessing Fusion Energy.

A stereotype is a commonly accepted but too-simple idea or belief about some thing or group. Stereotypes lump whole groups together based on a single trait. In cartooning, a stereotype is used to label figures easily recognized as members of groups. In this cartoon, for example, the two figures are scientists. Stereotypes of scientists often show them as older men, mostly bald but with a little frizzy hair, white coats, and so on.

Stereotypes make it easy to identify quickly the group a cartoon figure stands for. But some stereotypes may also be insulting. Over several weeks, find editorial cartoons with stereotypes of the groups listed below. Clip one cartoon for each group. Attach these cartoons to this sheet. Then to the right of each group's name, answer this question: Is the stereotype unfair? As a group, discuss the stereotypes in the cartoons and whether or not they are fair.

STEREOTYPE	IS THE STEREOTYPE UNFAIR?
old people	_____
young people	_____
African Americans	_____
Arabs	_____
businessmen	_____
politicians	_____

Caricature & Stereotype

Section 5 — Caricature & Stereotype — Activity #5

Caricatures make fun of personalities in the news by exaggerating or distorting one or more distinctive features of those personalities. But the best caricatures distort features in a way that reveals something important about the subject being caricatured. Look closely at these three caricatures of civil rights leader Jesse Jackson. Then answer the questions below.

Which caricature is most realistic? Why? _____
_____
_____

Which one is funniest? Why? _____
_____
_____

Which one is most distorted? Why? _____
_____
_____

Which one seems to reveal most about Mr. Jackson's personality? Why? _____
_____
_____

As a group, discuss your answers to these questions.

52 Understanding & Creating Editorial Cartoons

SECTION 6

CAPTIONS & OTHER WORDS

OBJECTIVES

The activities presented in this section are designed to help students see that words can be used in cartoons in a great many ways. These activities should also help your students understand that words work best in a cartoon when they reinforce the cartoon's nonverbal features. Words alone cannot do all the work of the cartoon.

COMMENTS

One of the biggest mistakes student cartoonists make is expecting words to do most of a cartoon's work. Take a look at the cartoons on the pages that follow. Cartoon #1, a student cartoon, is almost guilty of that mistake.

This cartoon comes close to being little more than a poster. As a poster, it would be clever and admirable, but a poster is not a cartoon. However, a few features in this cartoon save it and, in fact, make it quite good. The expression on the boy's face and the symbol of the trash can into which he is depositing his future add depth to what would otherwise be a simple verbal warning.

Often, students use such warnings ("smoking kills," "don't drink and drive," "save the Earth," etc.) as captions for very simple cartoons. Such captions are titles that actually give away the whole store. They make it unnecessary even to look at the visual elements in the cartoon. But the visual elements are what give the editorial cartoon its unique power.

After all, a cartoon can do without words entirely (As you see in Cartoon #2, a student-drawn cartoon). But words by themselves cannot make a complete cartoon-except in very rare cases, such as in Cartoon #3.

This "US-THEM" cartoon is only one dramatic example of the many ways words can work well in a cartoon. Cartoons can use captions, titles, famous sayings, or words uttered by one or more of the characters in the cartoon. Cartoon #4, another student cartoon, uses many words — and in two different ways — but it is still unified and it's given significance by the visual element of the public school building.

Cartoon #5 makes clear that even a simple one-word caption can suffice when it accompanies a vivid and powerful image.

Captions & Other Words

Section 6 — Captions & Other Words

ILLITERACY

KILLS OPPORTUNITY

CARTOON #1

Section 6 — Captions & Other Words

CARTOON #2

Section 6 — Captions & Other Words

CARTOON #3

56 — Understanding & Creating Editorial Cartoons

Section 6 — Captions & Other Words

CARTOON #4

Captions & Other Words

57

Section 6 — Captions & Other Words

"GESUNDHEIT"

CARTOON #5

58 Understanding & Creating Editorial Cartoons

Section 6 — Captions & Other Words — Activity #1

Look through your newspaper for a photo of top U.S. officials or other world leaders. Read the news story that goes with the photo. Attach the photo here. Then follow the directions underneath the space for the photo.

Write a caption for the photo that clearly states the main idea in the news story. _____
_____
_____

Write a caption that makes fun of one of the people in the photo. _____
_____
_____

Write a caption that makes a serious or angry point about the news story. _____
_____
_____

As a group, share your photo-cartoons and choose the best one. _____
_____
_____
_____

Section 6 — Captions & Other Words — Activity #2

Most cartoons have words. But not all of these words are in a caption. The cartoon above has a title, and it also uses words as objects in the cartoon's picture. Look closely at this cartoon. Then answer the following questions.

What does the cartoon title alone tell you this cartoon is about? _____
_____
_____
_____

In a war, what would you expect to see dropping out of the plane? _____
_____
_____
_____

What point do you think the artist is trying to make by showing all the "blah, blah, blahs" dropping out of the plane? _____
_____
_____
_____

On a separate sheet, draw this same cartoon, but leave out the "blah, blah, blahs." Instead, write your own caption for the cartoon. Do you think your caption makes the cartoon better or worse?

Section 6 — Captions & Other Words — Activity #3

Cartoons often use famous sayings, song lyrics, advertising slogans, and other well-known phrases as captions. Choose one of the phrases listed on the left below. Use it in an editorial cartoon of your own about one of the topics listed on the right.

Things go better with...	school violence
May the force be with you	Congress and the president
Truth or Dare	water pollution
Anything goes	homelessness
Just say no	abortion
Wheel of Fortune	gun control
Make my day	the Greenhouse Effect
Speak softly, but carry a big stick	TV violence

CAPTION _____

_____

_____

_____

Captions & Other Words

Section 6 — Captions & Other Words — Activity #4

Most editorial cartoons use words. Sometimes the words state the point of the cartoon in a very clear way. But in the best cartoons, the words only help the other parts of the cartoon make one overall point. In that way, the reader usually has to think harder about the cartoon and decide whether or not he or she agrees with its main point.

The student editorial cartoon above uses one very simple object — a voting booth — and a few words to make an important point. The words are "Election Booth" and a well-known rhyme. Study this cartoon closely and then answer the questions below.

What point is the cartoon making about the candidates in the election? _____
_____
_____

Make up a caption that could be used beneath the cartoon in place of the rhyme. _____
_____
_____

Do you think your caption makes the cartoon easier to understand? Why or why not? _____
_____
_____

Do you think your caption makes the cartoon better? Why or why not? _____
_____
_____

Section 6 — Captions & Other Words — Activity #5

Not all cartoons use words. The planet Earth is the main feature in both of these cartoons. But only one has a caption and other words. Study the two cartoons carefully. Then answer the questions below.

What is the main point of the cartoon on the left? _____
_____
_____

What is the main point of the cartoon on the right? _____
_____
_____

What words, if any, would you change if you were redoing the cartoon on the left? Why? _____
_____
_____

Do you think a caption would help or hurt the cartoon on the right? _____
_____
_____

Which cartoon makes its point most forcefully? Why? _____
_____
_____

Captions & Other Words

Section 6 — Captions & Other Words — Activity #6

The cartoon below uses just one word, the organization NATO, to make a very complicated point. To understand this cartoon, you need to know a good deal about NATO and about arguments between the U.S. and some European countries over NATO policy during the Cold War, and especially in the 1980s. You also need to think about the various symbols in the cartoon and about the way the letters in "NATO" are drawn. Read more about the arguments over NATO in the 1980s. Then answer the questions beneath the cartoon.

What complaint does the cartoon make about the attitudes of many Europeans toward NATO?
_____
_____
_____

What idea does the cartoonist get across by making the first three letters of "NATO" so thick and heavy-looking? _____
_____
_____

Why do you think the artist drew the letter "O" as a peace symbol on a balloon? _____
_____
_____
_____

How does the way "Europe" is drawn help the cartoon make its point? _____
_____
_____

64   Understanding & Creating Editorial Cartoons

SECTION 7

DRAWING & DESIGN

OBJECTIVES

The activities in this section are designed to make students more aware of some of the basic artistic techniques and rules of thumb that go into producing an effective editorial cartoon. These activities should help students avoid some of the most common difficulties young people get into when they first try to create their own editorial cartoons.

COMMENTS

The best editorial cartoons are likely to be both artistically sophisticated and intellectually challenging. You'll see some good examples of drawing, design, and composition on the next few pages. An ability to draw facial expressions, a sense of composition, an understanding of perspective, and a good feel for the use of sharp contrasts of black and white all make Cartoon #1 highly effective.

Most students don't have the skills to create highly artistic editorial cartoons. Fortunately, they don't have to — that is, unless they plan to make a career of editorial cartooning. To enjoy, understand, and draw effective editorial cartoons, students need only to keep a few points in mind.

Perhaps the most important of these points is to avoid cluttering up a cartoon with too many elements. Cartoon #2, a student cartoon, is a good example of a simple cartoon that makes a powerful statement. This is a well-drawn cartoon, but its effectiveness is really a result of its stark simplicity more than anything else.

Cartoon #3 is not at all sophisticated in an artistic sense. But it does make a clever comment about the economic rivalry between the U.S. and Japan. The student who drew this cartoon unified it both artistically and conceptually with the bombs on the left and the cars on the right. This conveys in an economical way, without words, the idea that trade might be a form of war by other means.

Again, all the words and visual elements in the cartoon work together to make a single point.

On the other hand, Cartoon #4, another student-drawn cartoon, is also simple and unified, but the words aren't clear. The cartoon's ironic humor could be lost as readers struggle to make out the words.

Here are a few simple rules of thumb that students should keep in mind as they sit down to create their own cartoons:

- Sketch first drafts of a cartoon lightly in pencil.
- Use pen or dark pencils for the final draft.
- Heavier and cleaner lines are usually preferable.
- Avoid clutter unless it is essential to the cartoon's point or meaning.
- Make sure the most important visual features stand out in some way.
- Keep objects in the correct proportions — exaggerate for a reason, but don't overdo it.
- Avoid too many words, and make sure the words are big enough and legible enough to be easily read.
- Keep action logical (remember people tend to "read" cartoons from left to right).

Section 7 — Drawing & Design

CARTOON #1

Understanding & Creating Editorial Cartoons

Section 7 — Drawing & Design

CARTOON #2

Drawing & Design

67

Section 7 — Drawing & Design

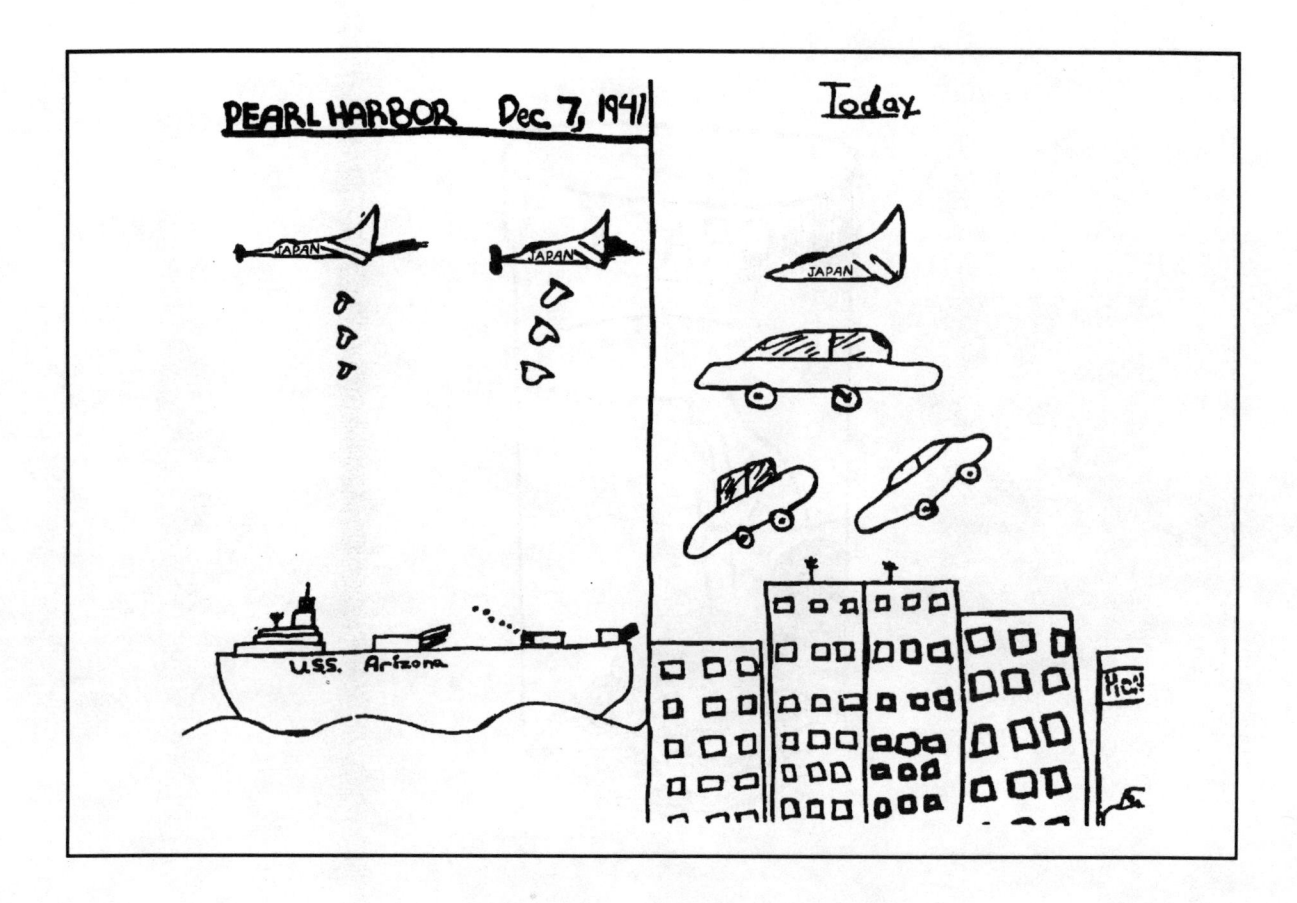

CARTOON #3

Understanding & Creating Editorial Cartoons

Section 7 — Drawing & Design

CARTOON #4

Drawing & Design 69

Section 7 — Drawing & Design — Activity #1

The sizes and shapes of all the objects in a cartoon should help make clear what that cartoon is about. Also, all the words in the cartoon should be clear and easy to read. Look through recent newspapers and cut out a number of editorial cartoons. Pick the one you think is drawn best. Attach it in the space below. Then answer the questions below.

What is the cartoon about? _____
_____
_____

Are the words in it clearly written? _____
_____
_____

What is the most important part of the cartoon? _____
_____
_____

What do you like most about the way the cartoon is drawn? _____
_____
_____

What parts, if any, would you change if you were drawing this cartoon? _____
_____
_____

Section 7 — Drawing & Design — Activity #2

This student-drawn cartoon is about students who are not learning enough in school. Most people who see this cartoon like it. But many of them say it is hard to understand at first. They say some parts are drawn well, but others are not. And they say it is not clear what parts of the cartoon the artist wants us to pay attention to most.

Try to make this cartoon better by redrawing it. Try to make the parts of the cartoon you think are important stand out more than they do now. Change the size or shape of its parts in any way you think best. You may want to shade the parts differently. Or you may decide to make the lines thinner or thicker. You could leave out some words, add others, or change the way the words are printed to make them clearer.

Drawing & Design

Section 7 — Drawing & Design — Activity #3

This cartoon does make a single point about a topic in the news: teenage curfews. The cartoon is in favor of such curfews. But it isn't easy to see that at first. Look closely at the cartoon and then answer the questions below.

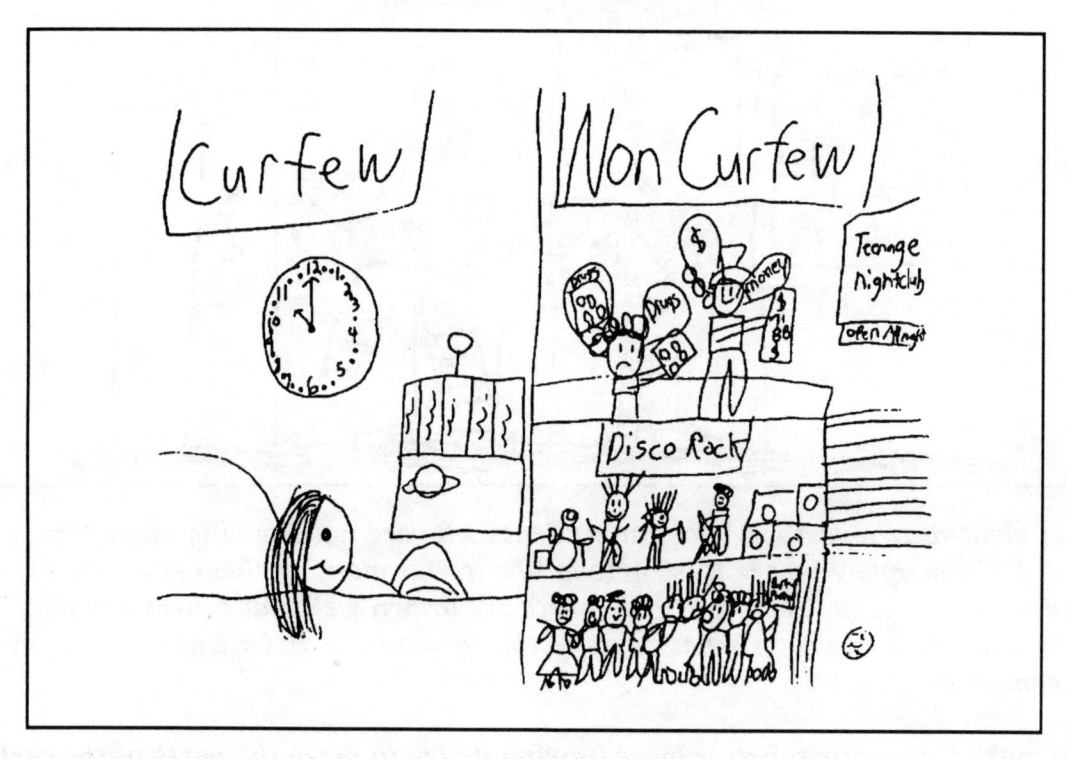

What big difference do you see between the left and right halves of the cartoon? _____
_____
_____

What parts of the cartoon help make the point that curfews are a good idea? _____
_____
_____

What parts of the cartoon could be left out? _____
_____
_____

What words, if any, would you change, leave out, or add? _____
_____

On a separate sheet of paper, redraw this cartoon to help make it better. _____
_____
_____

72   Understanding & Creating Editorial Cartoons

Section 7 — Drawing & Design — Activity #4

In some ways, this is a very simply drawn student editorial cartoon. But it makes a strong point about an ethical issue. Study the cartoon closely. Then answer the questions below.

In the space provided, explain what cloning is. _____
_____
_____

Why did the cartoonist use sheep in this cartoon? _____
_____
_____

Are the words "Noah's 20th Century Ark" good or bad words to use in this cartoon? Why? ____
_____
_____

What do you like or dislike about this cartoon? _____
_____
_____

Drawing & Design

Section 7 — Drawing & Design — Activity #5

Most people see this cartoon as a strong statement of outrage about the medical waste washing ashore on some of the nation's beaches. And yet it uses no words and makes no direct statement about the problem. It achieves its impact artistically. Study it closely. Then answer the questions below.

How does the position the little boy is in add to the emotion the cartoon arouses?
_____
_____
_____

Would it have helped or hurt the cartoon if more than a single syringe were shown on the beach? Why? _____
_____
_____

In what way does the lone sea gull add to the cartoon's impact? _____
_____
_____

In what way does the all-white background help enhance the cartoon's impact? _____
_____
_____

74   Understanding & Creating Editorial Cartoons

Section 7 — Drawing & Design — Activity #6

No matter how well-drawn a cartoon is, it must also be designed well. That is, each item in the cartoon should create some kind of visual balance, the items should seem related in a logical sequence or order, and there should be a sense of unity — even when one item stands out from the others. Look at this cartoon. Then in a brief paragraph below, explain what specific features in the cartoon help it attain balance, a sense of logical order, and unity.

The Great Escape — Part I

_____
_____
_____
_____
_____
_____
_____
_____
_____

Drawing & Design

SECTION 8

LITERARY & HISTORICAL REFERENCES

OBJECTIVES

The activities in this section are designed to make students aware of the wide range of historical, literary, and cultural materials cartoonists draw on for symbols and analogies, and to explain why these materials often provide the most powerful and economical images cartoons employ.

COMMENTS

As members of the same culture, we all share many common myths and symbols. In more traditional societies, these myths and symbols are transmitted primarily by a formal religious system. In our society, the sources are much more diverse — history, literature, fairy tales, movies television, even advertising.

Editorial cartoonists draw on all these sources for the images and ideas in their cartoons. In each case, an analogy is made between the symbol image, or myth in the cartoon and some present-day issue or event.

A famous phrase, a historical event, a myth, or a symbol can concisely capture our understanding about the past and our most strongly held beliefs and values. As an example, take the phrase "taxation without representation," which comes from the era of the American Revolution. This single phrase has a kind of mythic power because it expresses the deeply held views most Americans have about their nation's past and its particular strengths. It is this widely shared understanding that the cartoonist draws on in Cartoon #1, on the next page. He knows that people will understand the ironic implications of the wording change he makes in that famous phrase.

Take a look at the other cartoons that follow. Cartoon #2 also sparks this kind of immediate comprehension. It seeks to convey the idea that racial hatred is always present and often ready to re-emerge in new forms. Nothing symbolizes such hatred more effectively than the Nazi swastika. Over the years, thousands of cartoons have used this symbol for its dramatic effect. As with a phrase like "no taxation without representation," it concentrates a great deal of meaning into a single cartoon element.

In a way, that's the real value of symbols, events or images drawn from literature, history, and other sources. They are economizing devices. They make it possible to say a great deal and tease the reader with all sorts of implied parallels without giving away so much information as to become obvious.

Of course, to make such references work, the cartoonist must use them carefully. It's all too easy to misuse an analogy, either by distorting and oversimplifying a past episode, or by misapplying its lesson to a present-day event that differs substantially from the past episode. Of course, the critical analysis of such "false analogies" can itself be a valuable exercise for students.

The cartoonist must also be sure the myth or historical episode used is widely known and understood. Millions of people know the story of "The Wizard of Oz." But to understand the point it helps make in Cartoon #3, a reader would have to appreciate the significance of the story in a fairly sophisticated way. Cartoon #4 requires some knowledge of classical history and mythology, or at least a familiarity with the myth of Diogenes, who wandered the land in search of an honest man.

The point here is that the cartoonist must not only be sure of how to use any particular historical, literary, or other reference; he or she must also have a good sense of how widely shared and understood that reference is.

Section 8 — Literary & Historical References

CARTOON #1

Literary & Historical References 77

Section 8 — Literary & Historical References

CARTOON #2

78 — Understanding & Creating Editorial Cartoons

Section 8 — Literary & Historical References

CARTOON #3

Section 8 — Literary & Historical References

CARTOON #4

80   Understanding & Creating Editorial Cartoons

Section 8 — Literary & Historical References — Activity #1

Editorial cartoons often use famous people from history or characters from the Bible, other books, or even movies. Below is a list of a few famous people or characters.

       Abraham Lincoln
       Luke Skywalker and Darth Vader
       George Washington
       Superman
       Noah and his ark
       King Kong
       Little Red Riding Hood

Look through your newspaper for stories about important people in the news. List two of these news names below. In the space next to the name, draw a picture of that person as one of the figures in the list above. Make sure the historical or fictional characters you choose match in some way with the people you've chosen.

NEWS NAME #1

_____

NEWS NAME #2

_____

Literary & Historical References

Section 8 — Literary & Historical References — Activity #2

"Oh, look kids, isn't Joe cool?"

This cartoon uses the main figure in a group of cigarette ads to make a strong point about the dangers of smoking. Look through your newspaper or magazines for advertisements. Use one of these ads for ideas for an editorial cartoon of your own. Draw your cartoon in the space below. You may trace the parts of the ad you wish to use — but you may also change the ad in any way you wish. Attach the ad to this sheet.

Understanding & Creating Editorial Cartoons

Section 8 — Literary & Historical References — Activity #3

Many cartoons use events from history as a way to make a point about some current problem or event in the news. This cartoon is about a problem in our nation today. But to understand the cartoon, you need to know something about the historical event referred to in it. Study the cartoon and then answer the following questions.

> THE LOUISIANA PURCHASE, HUH? IT'S A LOT OF LAND BUT I GUESS IT COULD ALWAYS BE USED AS FUTURE DUMP SITES FOR THE EASTERN STATES.

What president made the Louisiana Purchase, and in what year did he make it? _____
_____
_____

From what nation did the U.S. buy lands included in the Louisiana Purchase? _____
_____
_____

What future states were formed from this territory? _____
_____
_____

What point do you think this cartoon is making? _____
_____
_____

How does the use of the Louisiana Purchase in this cartoon help it to make its point more forcefully? _____
_____
_____

Literary & Historical References

Section 8 — Literary & Historical References — Activity #4

Cartoons often use characters in books or movies to stand for people in the news today, or they copy scenes from those books or movies. Below is a list of well-known books and movies, or characters from books and movies.

> Huckleberry Finn
> The Terminator
> Indiana Jones
> E.T.
> Robinson Crusoe
> A Tale of Two Cities
> Star Wars
> Dr. Jekyll and Mr. Hyde
> Sherlock Holmes

Find an editorial or a news story about some big argument Americans are having now. Decide what your opinion is about the problem and the way important officials or other leaders are dealing with it. Then draw your own cartoon about this problem in the space below, using one of the characters or a scene from one of the books or movies listed here.

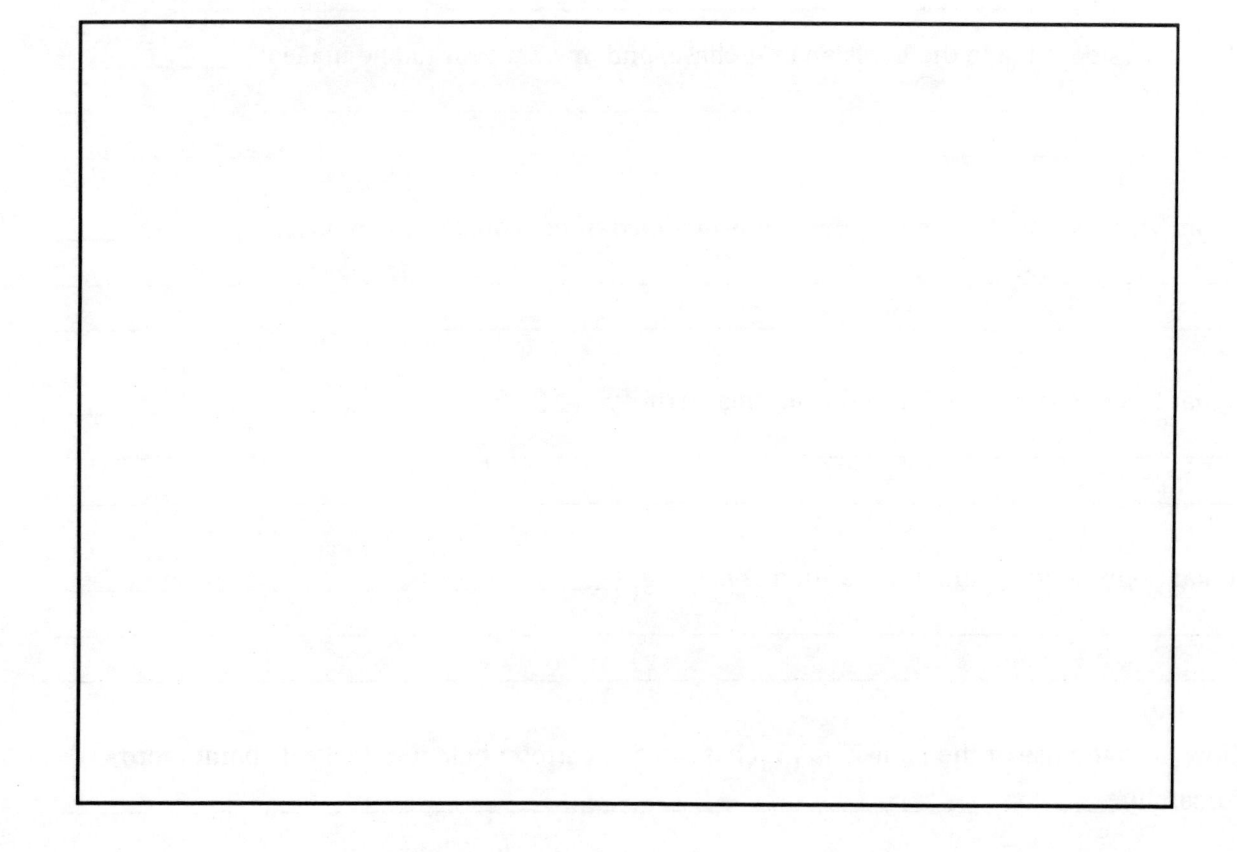

Section 8 — Literary & Historical References — Activity #5

In this cartoon, the figure of Neville Chamberlain is used to make a pointed attack on NATO's policy toward the civil war in Bosnia. Study the cartoon and answer these questions about it:

[Cartoon by MacNelly, Chicago Tribune. Caption reads: "NATO SENDS IN ITS CRACK NEVILLE CHAMBERLAIN DIVISION:" showing a group of top-hatted men cheering beside a large tank labeled "SERBIA" with a skull and crossbones.]

Briefly sum up the nature of the conflict in Bosnia. Explain why the tank in this cartoon is labeled "Serbia." _____
_____
_____

Identify Neville Chamberlain and explain briefly the impact his diplomatic efforts had on European history in the late 1930s. _____
_____
_____

What point is the cartoon making, and how does the figure of Neville Chamberlain help it to make that point? _____
_____
_____

Literary & Historical References

Section 8 — Literary & Historical References — Activity #6

Cartoonists often use famous historical phrases or quotations to good effect in their editorial cartoons. These phrases are effective because they are recognizable, but cartoonists often reuse the phrases in ways that go far beyond the original meaning of the words. Take a look at the famous quotes below.

"One small step for man, one giant leap for mankind."

"Ask not what your country can do for you, ask what you can do for your country."

"Of the people, by the people, for the people."

"I shall return."

"This was their finest hour."

Use one of these famous quotes as a caption or title for a cartoon about some current issue in the news. Draw your cartoon in the space provided.

SECTION 9

CARTOONS & HISTORY

OBJECTIVES

The activities in this section are designed to teach students to appreciate editorial cartoons as valuable sources of information about earlier periods of history. Students should come to see that the editorial cartoon, as a popular art from with mass appeal, often evokes the spirit or temper of a time better than many other primary historical sources.

COMMENTS

Editorial cartoons have played a major role in our country's history. You can see examples of them on the next pages. Editorial cartoons were around even before the founding of the republic, as Cartoon #1 by Benjamin Franklin makes clear.

It's safe to say that no artist draws a cartoon with the expectation that it will survive and be of lasting historical interest. Cartoons are comments on the passing scene. They are meant to affect public debate about an issue while that issue is still alive and unsettled. And yet this is just what makes editorial cartoons so valuable as historical documents. They are a unique window into a moment in the past as it appeared to people living in it.

As such, editorial cartoons from the past are often hard to interpret. They assume a fund of background knowledge that, almost by definition, is bound to fade or alter rapidly over time. As a result, they are often a kind of modern-day hieroglyphics, riddles that can only be solved by research and historical detective work.

Think, for example, of the kinds of background knowledge a student would have to acquire in order to correctly explain all the nuances in Cartoon #2, drawn by the late 19th century cartoonist Frederick Opper. This cartoon makes a comment on President Grover Cleveland and his intentions to cut the highly protective tariff of his day.

As experts on the editorial cartoon, your students should now be in a position to do the kind of detective work required to explain such cartoons. And this could be an enjoyable way to unravel all sorts of mysteries about the past debates and controversies that have shaped our republic.

Cartoons & History 87

Section 9— Cartoons & History

CARTOON #1

Section 9— Cartoons & History

DOCTOR CLEVELAND'S PATIENTS.
"Uncle Sam (to Civil Service Reform) — Don't cry, my child, he'll look after you presently. Your brother needs attention more than you do."

CARTOON #2

Cartoons & History 89

Section 9— Cartoons & History — Activity #1

For many years, the figure of Uncle Sam has been used in editorial cartoons to stand for the United States. Above are three examples of Uncle Sam from cartoons and posters in the past. What do you think the Uncle Sam of the future might look like? Use the space below to draw your own Uncle Sam for the 21st century.

Understanding & Creating Editorial Cartoons

Section 9— Cartoons & History — Activity #2

Over the next two weeks, collect all the editorial cartoons you can find. Divide them into two lists. Make one list for the cartoons that do not mention people or events from history. Make another list for those that do mention people or events from history. Which list is longer?

Choose one cartoon that uses some person or event from our nation's history. Attach that cartoon in the space below. Read more about the people or events in history that the cartoon shows. Now, in a sentence or two, explain what the cartoon is about and why it uses people or events from past history.

_____
_____
_____
_____
_____
_____
_____
_____
_____
_____
_____
_____

Section 9— Cartoons & History — Activity #3

This famous cartoon was drawn by Benjamin Franklin in 1754. Using history textbooks, encyclopedias, and other sources, learn more about Benjamin Franklin and about what was happening in the British colonies of North America in that year. Based on your reading, answer the questions below.

JOIN, or DIE.

What does each piece of the snake stand for? _____
_____
_____

Why did Franklin show this snake divided into pieces? _____
_____
_____

What specific events do you think he had in mind when he drew this cartoon? _____
_____
_____

What point is the cartoon trying to make? _____
_____
_____

Section 9— Cartoons & History — Activity #4

Americans have argued over many issues at one time or another. A few of these important issues are listed below.

> The abolition of slavery
> The right of women to vote
> Child labor
> America's decision to enter World War One
> Franklin Roosevelt's "New Deal"

Use history textbooks and other sources to learn more about one of these big arguments. Pretend you are an editorial cartoonist at the time the argument you researched was taking place. In the space below, draw your own editorial cartoon about that argument.

Cartoons & History

Section 9— Cartoons & History — Activity #5

This famous cartoon by David Low is about a very important event that took place in Europe in 1939. Read history textbooks or encyclopedia articles to learn more about that famous event. Then in a brief paragraph, explain the cartoon. In your explanation, be sure to answer this question: Why do the words attributed to the two figures in the cartoon make it so heavily ironic?

____

94   Understanding & Creating Editorial Cartoons

Section 9— Cartoons & History — Activity #6

This cartoon from the late 1800s comments on the relationship between economic and political power. Read more about what was happening in the late 1800s in the United States. Based on your reading, explain the cartoon. Do you think this cartoon is still relevant to problems in our political system today? Why or why not?

"THE TRUST GIANT'S POINT OF VIEW"

Bibliography

Becker, Stephen D. *Comic Art in America*. New York: Simon & Schuster, 1959.

Block, Herbert *The Herb Block Gallery*. New York: Simon & Schuster, 1968.

Butt, William S., ed. *Hugh Haynie: Perspective*. Louisville. Published by The Courier-Journal and The Louisville Times, 1974.

Caket, Colin *Drawing Cartoons*. Poole, Dorset: Blandford Press, 1982.

Campbell, Mary and Gordon *The Pen, Not the Sword*. Nashville: Aurora, 1970.

Foreign Policy Association *Cartoon History of Foreign Policy, 1776-1976*. New York: William Morrow, 1975.

Gould, Ann, ed., *Masters of Caricature*. New York: Knopf, 1981.

Hoff, Syd *The Art of Cartooning*. New York: Stravon Educational Press, 1973.

Kelly, Walt *Ten Ever-Lovin' Blue-Eyed Years with Pogo*. New York: Simon & Schuster, 1959.

_____ *Walt Kelly's Pogo Revisited*. New York: Simon & Schuster, 1959.

Ketchum, Alton *Uncle Sam: The Man and the Legend*. New York: Hill and Wang, 1959.

Levine, David *The Art of David Levine*. New York: Knopf, 1978.

Low, David *Years of Wrath: A Cartoon History, 1931-1945*. New York: Simon & Schuster, 1946.

Mauldin, Bill *Up Front*. New York: Henry Holt & Co., 1945.

Oliphant, Pat *An Informal Gathering*. New York: Simon & Schuster, 1978.

Paine, Albert B. *Thomas Nast*. New York: Chelsea House, 1980.

Thomson, Ross and Bill Hewison *How to Draw and Sell Cartoons*. Cincinnati: North Light, 1985.